Lessons on Demand Presents

Teacher Guide and Novel Unit for

Salt to the Sea

By:

John Pennington

The lessons on demand series is designed to provide ready to use resources for novel study. In this book you will find key vocabulary, student organizer pages, and assessments.

This guide is divided into two sections. Section one is the teacher section which consists of vocabulary and activities. Section two holds all of the student pages, including assessments and graphic organizers.

Now available! Student Workbooks!

Find them on Amazon.com

Section One

Teacher Pages

Vocabulary

Suggested Activities

Chapters 1—17 Vocabulary

Guilt

Conscience

Evacuation

Deserter

Fate

Fatigued

Shame

Valor

Extermination

Indignity

Refugees

Massacre

Chapters 1-17 Activities

Reading Check Question / Quiz:

When does this story take place? A few years after 1941

How does Florian attempt to clean his wound? Vodka from the Russian

Who joins Joana's group at the abandon house? Florian and Emila

What does Joan tell Florian after the surgery? I'm a murderer

Blooms Higher Order Question:

Create a chart listing groups that show groups that are oppressors and victims

Suggested Activity Sheets (see Section Two):

Character Sketch—Joana

Character Sketch—Florian

Character Sketch—Emila

Character Sketch—Alfred Frick

Research Connection—Prussia

Research Connection—Lithuania

Research Connection—Hitler

Research Connection—Stalin

Draw the Scene

Who, What, When, Where and How

Chapters 17-50 Vocabulary

Restoration

Philosophy

Observation

Meticulous

Recitation

Evaluation

Demeanor

Taut

Lithe

Ambitious

Aristocrat

Evacuation

Chapters 17-50 Activities

Reading Check Question / Quiz:

Who did Florian steal from before leaving the abandon house after the surgery? Joana

What did the Shoe Poet lead the group to? An Estate

What had been the cause of Emilia's suffering? She was eight months pregnant

Who had killed the family of the estate? The grandfather

Blooms Higher Order Question:

Compile a list, using Alfred's song, of all the types of people persecuted by the Nazis. Determine if those groups are still being persecuted by your government.

Suggested Activity Sheets (see Section Two):

Character Sketch—Shoe Poet

Character Sketch—Eve

Character Sketch—Ingrid

Research Connection—Jew

Research Connection—Mein Kampf

Research Connection—Communist

Research Connection—Copernicus

Precognition Sheet

What Would You Do?

Chapters 51-103 Vocabulary

Euphoria

Hysteria

Provisions

Trauma

Stethoscope

Obliged

Infidel

Manipulate

Pandemonium

Ensued

Gullible

Aptitude

Chapters 51-103 Activities

Reading Check Question / Quiz:

Who fell through the ice when the group was trying to cross? Ingrid

Why did Joana get a pass before everyone else? Nurses were needed for the sick and wounded

Why did Eva not go with the others to get a pass? She was unwilling to leave her possessions

What did Emilia believe would happen to her when she had the baby? She would die

Blooms Higher Order Question:

Rank the priority of people allowed on the boat, create your own list and compare the two lists.

Suggested Activity Sheets (see Section Two):

Research Connection—Amber Room

Research Connection— Baltic Sea

Research Connection—Florence Nightingale

Research Connection—Typhus

Research Connection—Ghetto

Research Connection—Julian Falat

Create the Test

Interview

Top Ten List—Events

Write a Letter

Chapters 104-End Vocabulary

Mongrel

Camouflage

Regime

Suspicious

Inspection

Virtuous

Insipid

Confetti

Hypothermia

Panorama

Catastrophe

Synagogue

<u>Reading Check Question / Quiz:</u>

What happened to Florian's father? He was hung for making maps to help assassinate Hitler

What did Emilia do when offered the last spot on the boat? Sent the Wandering Boy

What characters survived? Joana, Florian, Wandering Boy, Halinka (Emilia's baby)

What happened to the Amber Room? No one had found the missing artifacts

<u>Blooms Higher Order Question:</u>

Create a chart that compares statistics from 5 famous boats that sank.

Chapter Vocabulary

Chapter Activities

Reading Check Question / Quiz:

Blooms Higher Order Question:

Suggested Activity Sheets (see Section Two):

Discussion Questions

Section Two

Student Work Pages

Work Pages

Graphic Organizers

Assessments

Activity Descriptions

Advertisement—Select an item from the text and have the students use text clues to draw an advertisement about that item.

Chapter to Poem—Students select 20 words from the text to write a five line poem with 3 words on each line.

Character Sketch—Students complete the information about a character using text clues.

Comic Strip— Students will create a visual representation of the chapter in a series of drawings.

Compare and Contrast—Select two items to make relationship connections with text support.

Create the Test—have the students use the text to create appropriate test questions.

Draw the Scene—students use text clues to draw a visual representation of the chapter.

Interview— Students design questions you would ask a character in the book and then write that characters response.

Lost Scene—Students use text clues to decide what would happen after a certain place in the story.

Making Connections—students use the text to find two items that are connected and label what kind of relationship connects them.

Precognition Sheet—students envision a character, think about what will happen next, and then determine what the result of that would be.

Activity Descriptions

Pyramid—Students use the text to arrange a series of items in an hierarchy format.

Research Connection—Students use an outside source to learn more about a topic in the text.

Sequencing—students will arrange events in the text in order given a specific context.

Support This! - Students use text to support a specific idea or concept.

Travel Brochure—Students use information in the text to create an informational text about the location

Top Ten List—Students create a list of items ranked from 1 to 10 with a specific theme.

Vocabulary Box—Students explore certain vocabulary words used in the text.

What Would You Do? - Students compare how characters in the text would react and compare that with how they personally would react.

Who, What, When, Where, and How—Students create a series of questions that begin with the following words that are connected to the text.

Write a Letter—Students write a letter to a character in the text.

Activity Descriptions (for scripts and poems)

Add a Character—Students will add a character that does not appear in the scene and create dialog and responses from other characters.

Costume Design—Students will design costumes that are appropriate to the characters in the scene and explain why they chose the design.

Props Needed— Students will make a list of props they believe are needed and justify their choices with text.

Soundtrack! - Students will create a sound track they believe fits the play and justify each song choice.

Stage Directions— Students will decide how the characters should move on, around, or off stage.

Poetry Analysis—Students will determine the plot, theme, setting, subject, tone and important words and phrases.

NAME:

TEACHER:

Date:

Advertisement: Draw an advertisement for the book

Chapter to Poem

Assignment: Select 20 words found in the chapter to create a poem where each line is 3 words long.

Title:

_____ _____ _____

_____ _____ _____

_____ _____ _____

_____ _____ _____

_____ _____ _____

NAME:

TEACHER:

Date:

Character Sketch

Name

Draw a picture

Personality/ Distinguishing marks

Connections to other characters

Important Actions

NAME:

TEACHER:

Date:

Comic Strip

Compare and Contrast
Venn Diagram

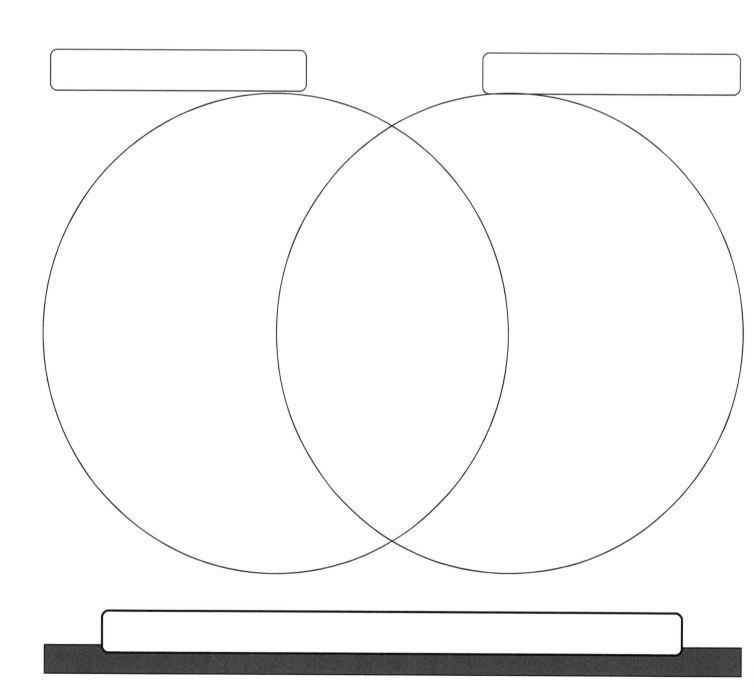

Create the Test

Question:

Answer:

Question:

Answer:

Question:

Answer:

Question:

Answer:

NAME:

TEACHER:

Date:

Draw the Scene: What five things have you included in the scene?

1   2   3

4   5

NAME:

TEACHER:

Date:

Interview: Who _____

Question:

Answer:

Question:

Answer:

Question:

Answer:

Question:

Answer:

NAME:

TEACHER:

Date:

Lost Scene: Write a scene that takes place between _____ and
_____

Making Connections

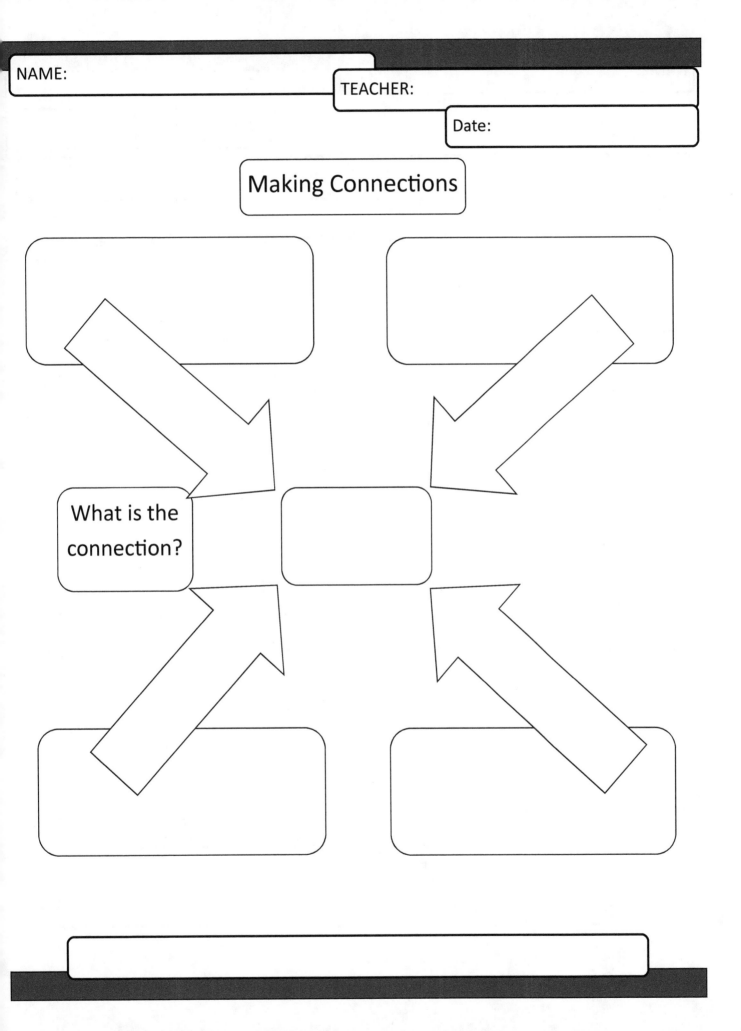

What is the connection?

NAME:

TEACHER:

Date:

Precognition Sheet

Who ?

What's going to happen?

What will be the result?

Who ?

What's going to happen?

What will be the result?

Who ?

What's going to happen?

What will be the result?

Who ?

What's going to happen?

What will be the result?

How many did you get correct?

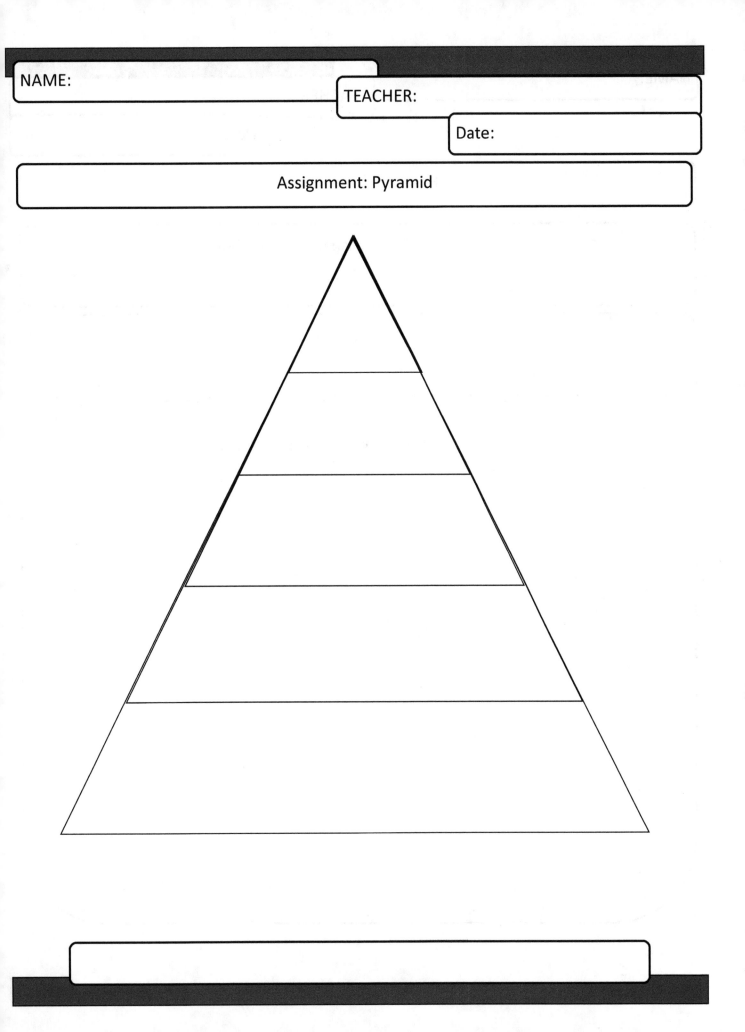

NAME:

TEACHER:

Date:

Assignment: Pyramid

NAME:

TEACHER:

Date:

Research connections

Source (URL, Book, Magazine, Interview)

What am I researching?

Facts I found that could be useful or notes

1.

2.

3.

4.

5.

6.

NAME:

TEACHER:

Date:

Sequencing or timeline

1.

2.

3.

4.

5.

NAME:

TEACHER:

Date:

Support This!

Supporting text

What page?

Supporting text

What page?

Central idea or statement

_____

Supporting text

What page?

Supporting text

What page?

NAME:

TEACHER:

Date:

Travel Brochure

Why should you visit?

Map

What are you going to see?

Special Events

Top Ten List

1.

2.

3.

4.

5.

6.

7.

8.

9.

10.

NAME:

TEACHER:

Date:

Vocabulary Box

Definition:

Draw:

Word:

Related words:

Use in a sentence:

Definition:

Draw:

Word:

Related words:

Use in a sentence:

What would you do?

Character: _____

What did they do?

Example from text:

What would you do?

Why would that be better?

Character: _____

What did they do?

Example from text:

What would you do?

Why would that be better?

Character: _____

What did they do?

Example from text:

What would you do?

Why would that be better?

NAME:

TEACHER:

Date:

Who, What, When, Where, and How

Who

What

Where

When

How

NAME:

TEACHER:

Date:

Write a letter

To:

From:

NAME:

TEACHER:

Date:

Assignment:

Add a Character

Who is the new character?

What reason does the new character have for being there?

Write a dialog between the new character and characters currently in the scene.

You dialog must be 6 lines or more, and can occur in the beginning, middle or end of the scene.

Costume Design

Draw a costume for one the characters in the scene.

Why do you believe this character should have a costume like this?

NAME:

TEACHER:

Date:

Props Needed

Prop:

What text from the scene supports this?

Prop:

What text from the scene supports this?

Prop:

What text from the scene supports this?

NAME:

TEACHER:

Date:

Soundtrack!

Song:

Why should this song be used?

Song:

Why should this song be used?

Song:

Why should this song be used?

TEACHER:

Date:

Stage Directions

List who is moving, how they are moving and use text from the dialog to determine when they move.

Who:

How:

When:

Who:

How:

When:

Who:

How:

When:

NAME:

TEACHER:

Poetry Analysis

Date:

Name of Poem:

Subject:

Text Support:

Plot:

Text Support:

Theme:

Text Support:

Setting:

Text Support:

Tone:

Text Support:

Important Words and Phrases:

Why are these words and phrases important:

Printed in the USA
CPSIA information can be obtained
at www.ICGtesting.com
LVHW060728090923
757723LV00017B/1151